INSPIRE

HAIR FASHION FOR SALON CLIENTS

Salon Fluxx
HAIR: Rachel Plimpton
COLOR: Mya Santoyo
MAKEUP: Jill Gosser
PHOTO: Steven Ledell

INSPIRE
HAIR FASHION FOR SALON CLIENTS

Featuring MEN'S STYLES

Table of Contents Volume 84

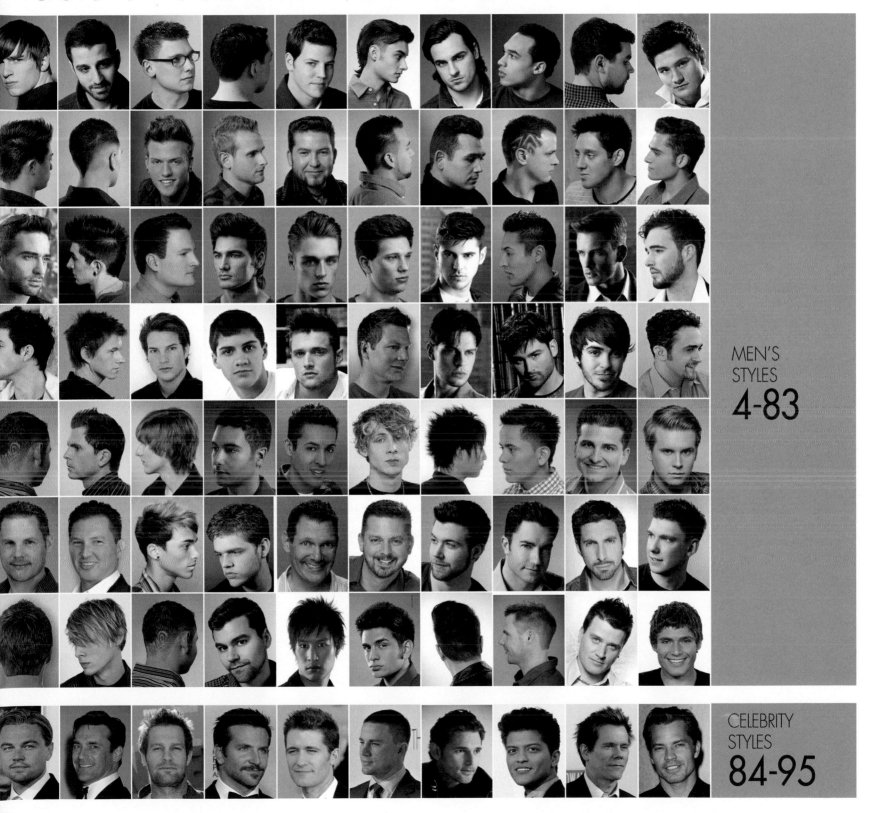

Diadema Hair Fashion
HAIR: X-men
MAKEUP: Cristina Marzo per Diadema
PHOTO: Stefano Bidini

4

Ladies & Gentlemen Salon & Spa
HAIR: Vanessa Loebsack for Ladies & Gentlemen
Salon & Spa, Cleveland, OH
PHOTO: Tom Carson

Ladies & Gentlemen Salon & Spa
HAIR: David Pavesich for Ladies & Gentlemen
Salon & Spa, Cleveland, OH
PHOTO: Tom Carson

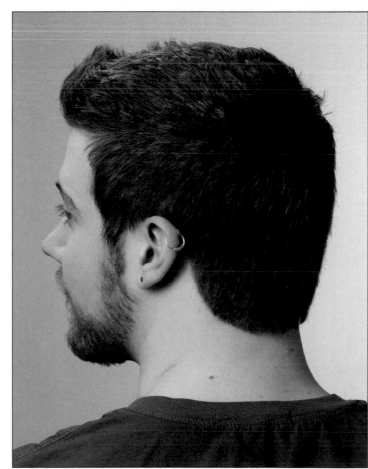

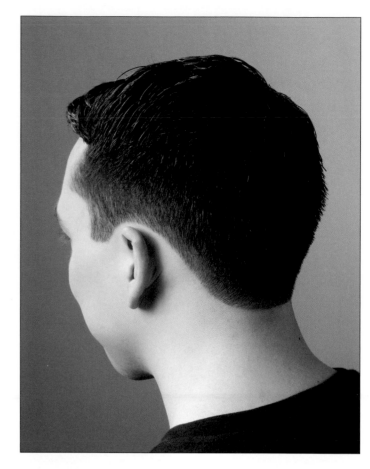

Ladies & Gentlemen Salon & Spa
HAIR: Katie Reis for Ladies &
Gentlemen Salon & Spa,
Cleveland, OH
PHOTO: Tom Carson

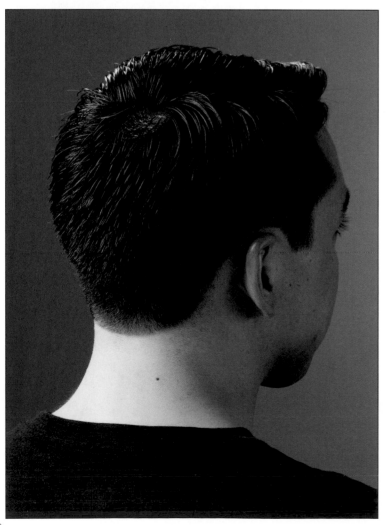

Ladies & Gentlemen Salon & Spa
HAIR: Michael Pavlick for Ladies & Gentlemen
Salon & Spa, Cleveland, OH
PHOTO: Tom Carson

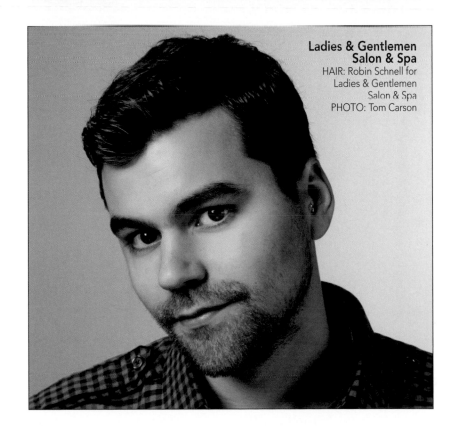

Ladies & Gentlemen
Salon & Spa
HAIR: Robin Schnell for
Ladies & Gentlemen
Salon & Spa
PHOTO: Tom Carson

Great Clips
HAIR: Hairstyle by Great Clips
PHOTO: Tom Carson

Designing Minds Salon
HAIR: Erica Miller Shuglie
PHOTO: Jeffrey James Miller

Visible Changes
HAIR: Visible Changes Artistic Team
PHOTO: Teddy Tran

Pivot Point International
HAIR: George Accatato/
Educational Consultant
MAKEUP: Rommy Najor
PHOTO: David Placek

Visible Changes
HAIR: Visible Changes
Artistic Team
PHOTO: Teddy Tran

Visible Changes
HAIR: Visible Changes
Artistic Team
PHOTO: Teddy Tran

Fusion Salon
HAIR: Jes Sutton
MAKEUP: Jes Sutton
PHOTO: Tyler Lewis

Fusion Salon
HAIR: Jes Sutton
MAKEUP: Jes Sutton
PHOTO: Tyler Lewis

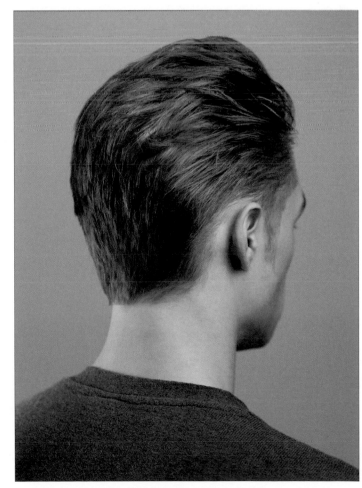

Salon Renaissance
HAIR: Debra Barnard
MAKEUP: Debra Barnard
PHOTO: Matt Deverman,
Chris Deverman

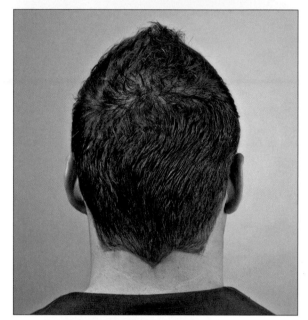

Salon Renaissance
HAIR: Debra Barnard
MAKEUP: Debra Barnard
PHOTO: Matt Doverman,
Chris Deverman

Diadema Hair Fashion
HAIR: X-men
MAKEUP: Cristina Marzo per Diadema
PHOTO: Stefano Bidini

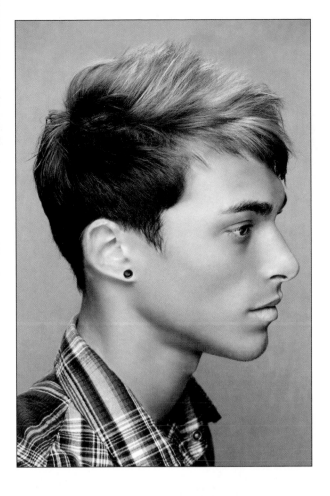

Michael's Salon & Spa
HAIR: James Wray
MAKEUP: James Wray
PHOTO: Michael Schuh,
The Media Group
at Michael's Salon &
Moto Photo

Fantastic Sams-Corona, CA
HAIR: Magda Nieblas
PHOTO: Taggart Winterhalter
for Purely Visual

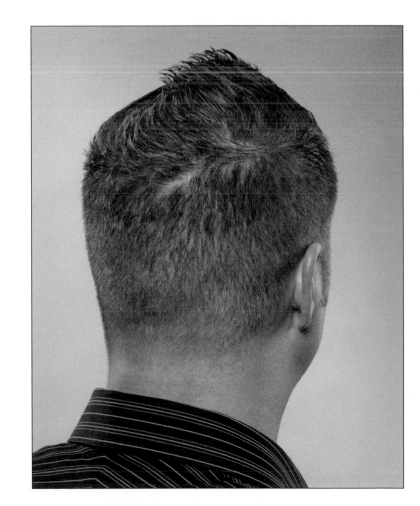

17

Timeless Creations Salon & Spa
HAIR: Christina McKelvey
MAKEUP: Alice Heilsen
PHOTO: Christopher Bright

Great Clips
HAIR: Hairstyle by Great Clips
PHOTO: Tom Carson

Ladies & Gentlemen Salon & Spa
HAIR: Alissa Archacki for
Ladies & Gentlemen Salon & Spa,
Cleveland, OH
PHOTO: Tom Carson

Great Clips
HAIR: Hairstyle by Great Clips
PHOTO: Tom Carson

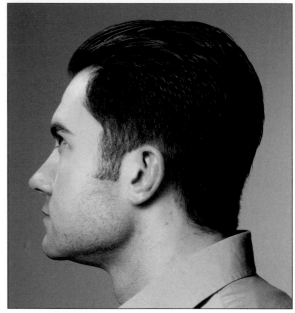

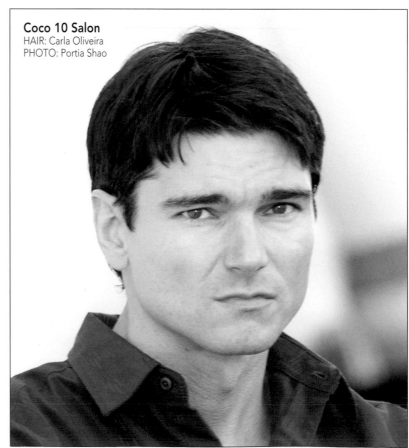

Diadema Hair Fashion
HAIR: X-men
MAKEUP: Cristina Marzo per Diadema
PHOTO: Stefano Bidini

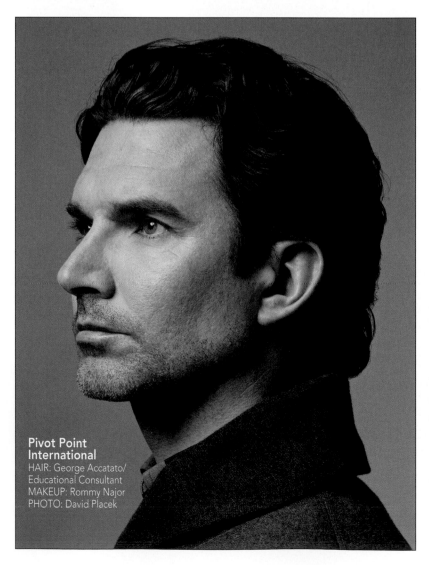

MEN'S STYLES

ENJOY Hair Care
HAIR: Patrick Dockry
PHOTO: Allen Carrasco

Fantastic Sams-Riverside, CA
HAIR: Lily Dalou
PHOTO: Taggart Winterhalter
for Purely Visual

Ladies & Gentlemen Salon & Spa
HAIR: Michael Pavlick for
Ladies & Gentlemen Salon & Spa,
Cleveland, OH
PHOTO: Tom Carson

Diadema Hair Fashion
HAIR: X-men
MAKEUP: Cristina Marzo per Diadema
PHOTO: Stefano Bidini

26

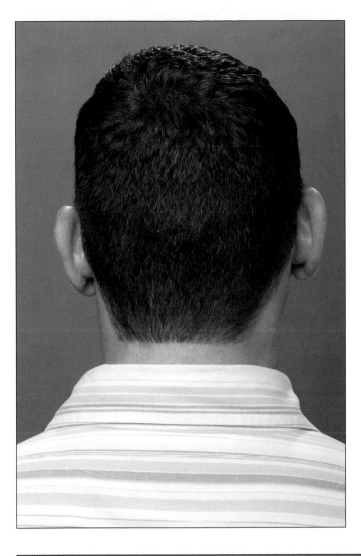

Creative Age
PHOTO: Armando Sanchez

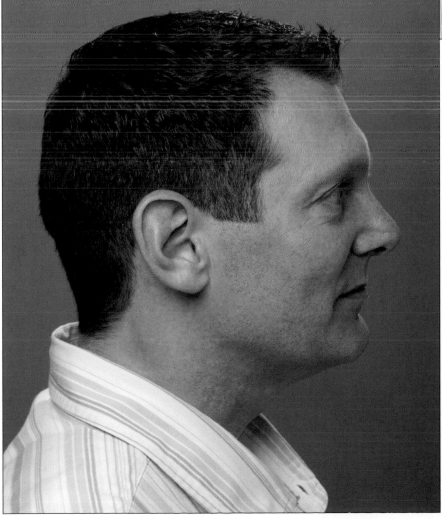

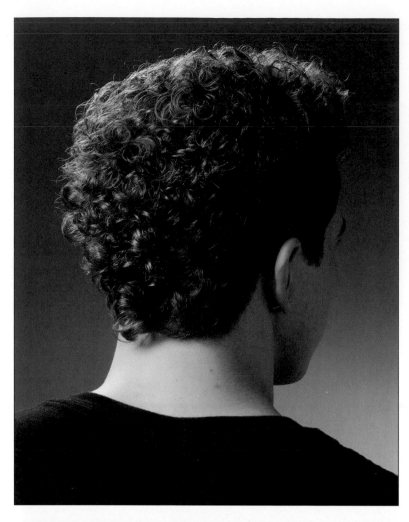

Ladies & Gentlemen Salon & Spa
HAIR: Katie Baxter for
Ladies & Gentlemen Salon & Spa,
Cleveland, OH
PHOTO: Tom Carson

Great Clips
HAIR: Hairstyle by
Great Clips
PHOTO: Tom Carson

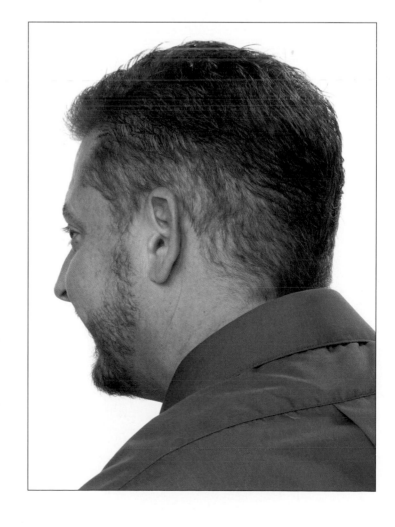

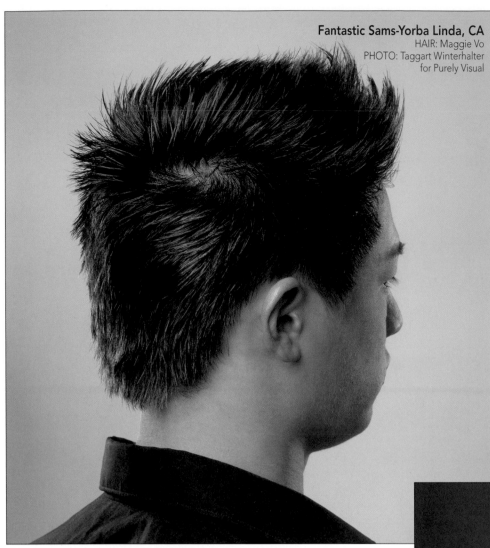

Fantastic Sams-Yorba Linda, CA
HAIR: Maggie Vo
PHOTO: Taggart Winterhalter
for Purely Visual

Salon Renaissance
HAIR: Debra Barnard
MAKEUP: Debra Barnard
PHOTO: Matt Deverman,
Chris Deverman

Great Clips
HAIR: Hairstyle by Great Clips
PHOTO: Tom Carson

Great Clips
HAIR: Hairstyle by
Great Clips
PHOTO: Tom Carson

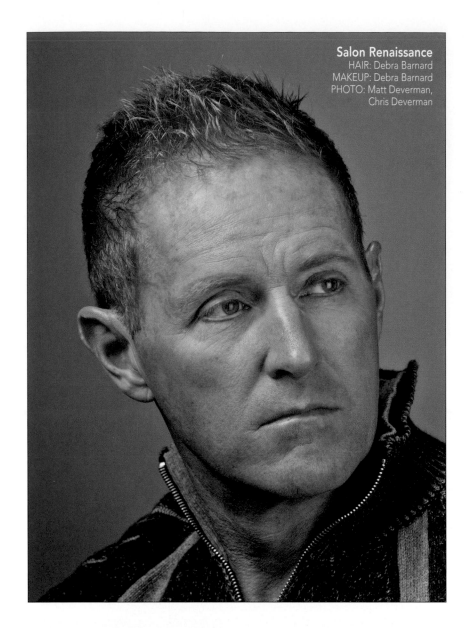

Salon Renaissance
HAIR: Debra Barnard
MAKEUP: Debra Barnard
PHOTO: Matt Deverman,
Chris Deverman

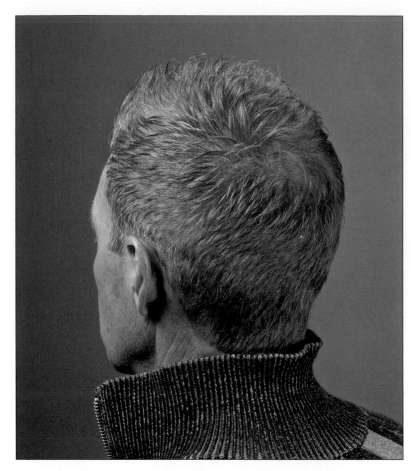

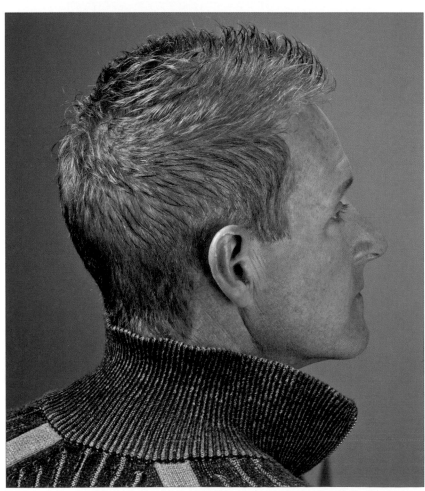

Fantastic Sams-Corona, CA
HAIR: Tina Vraneza
PHOTO: Taggart Winterhalter
for Purely Visual

**Ladies & Gentlemen
Salon & Spa**
HAIR: Lou Belknap for
Ladies & Gentlemen
Salon & Spa,
Cleveland, OH
PHOTO: Tom Carson

Fusion Salon
HAIR: Jes Sutton
MAKEUP: Jes Sutton
PHOTO: Tyler Lewis

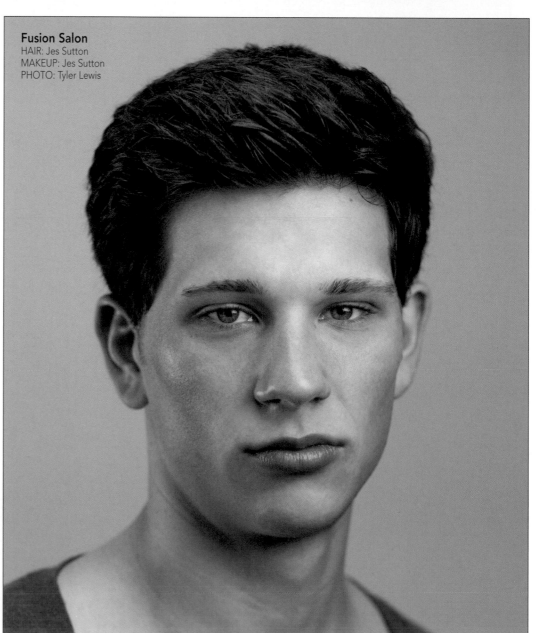

Diadema Hair Fashion
HAIR: X-men
MAKEUP: Cristina Marzo per Diadema
PHOTO: Stefano Bidini

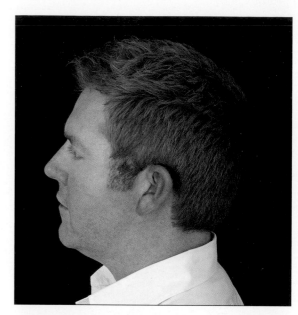

Bangs Salon & Studio
HAIR: Memory Fiola
PHOTO: Memory Fiola

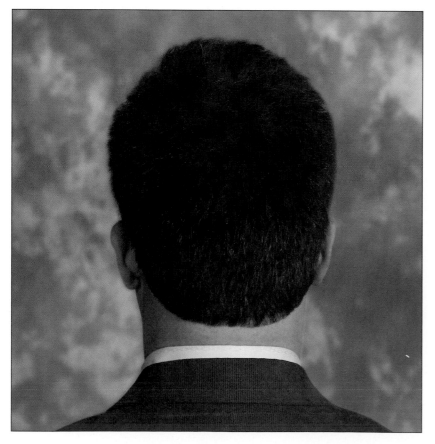

What's New The Salon
HAIR: Lindsey Haynes
PHOTO: Daphayne Chrisman

36

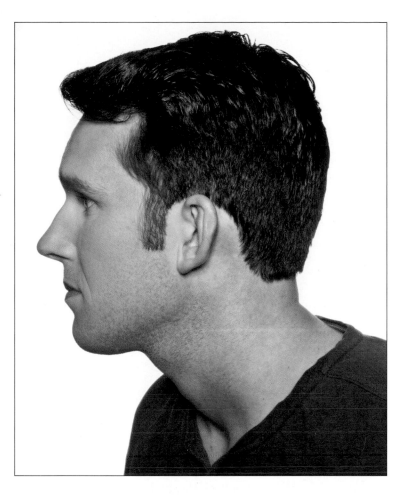

Modern Concepts Salon
HAIR: Margaret Murphy
MAKEUP: Wahyda Kochay
PHOTO: Javier Pierrend

Modern Concepts Salon
HAIR: Margaret Murphy
PHOTO: Javier Pierrend

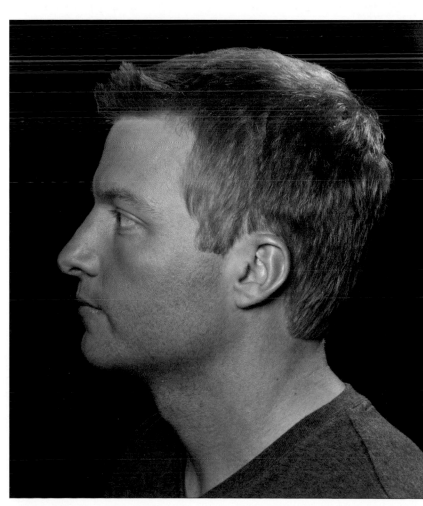

Ladies & Gentlemen Salon & Spa
HAIR: Shawna Partin for
Ladies & Gentlemen Salon & Spa
PHOTO: Tom Carson

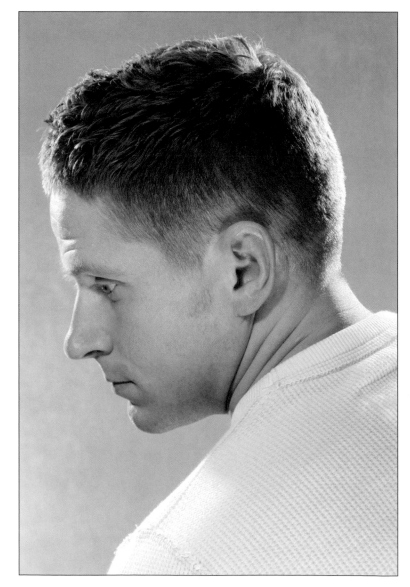

Ladies & Gentlemen Salon & Spa
HAIR: Shawna Partin for
Ladies & Gentlemen Salon & Spa,
Cleveland, OH
PHOTO: Tom Carson

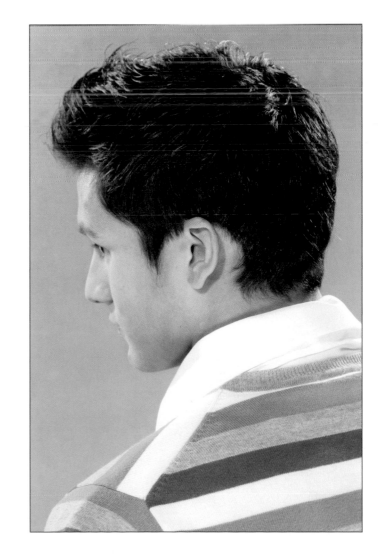

**Ladies & Gentlemen
Salon & Spa**
HAIR: Shawna Partin for
Ladies & Gentlemen
Salon & Spa,
Cleveland, OH
PHOTO: Tom Carson

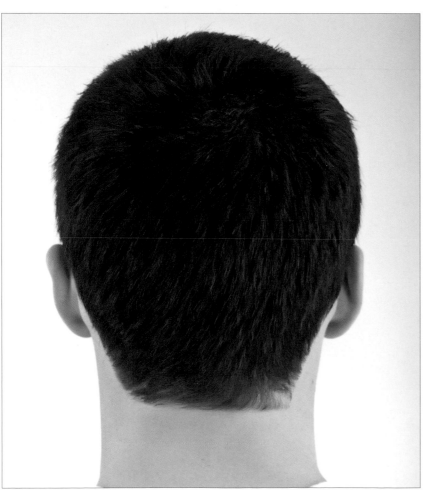

Hair Experience
HAIR: Sherene Collins
PHOTO: Pete Albert

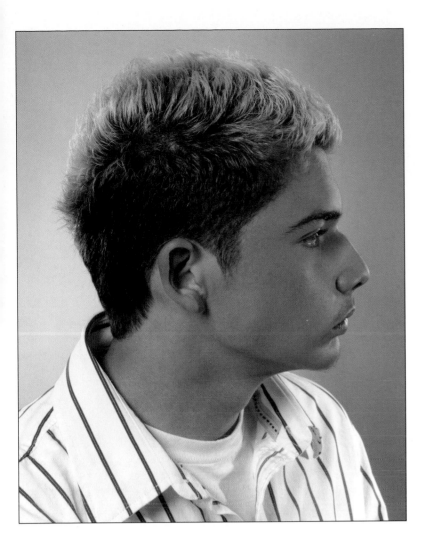

Fantastic Sams-Norco, CA
HAIR: Jessica Sanchez
PHOTO: Taggart Winterhalter
for Purely Visual

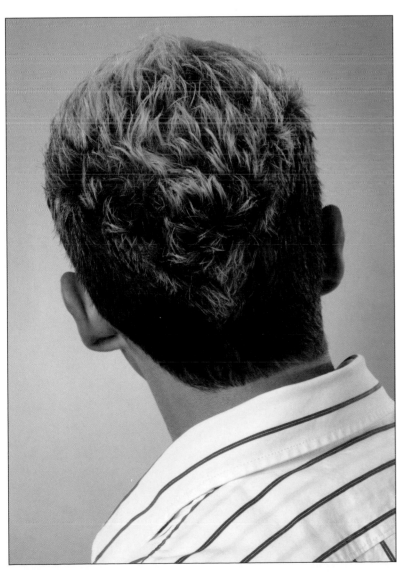

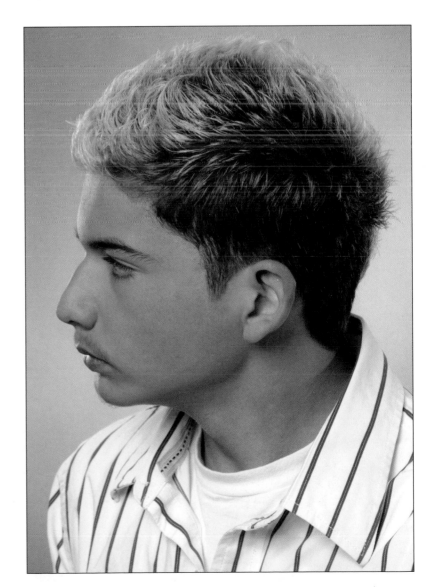

GAGE FOR MEN
HAIR: Antonio Cutrone
PHOTO: Ed Brown

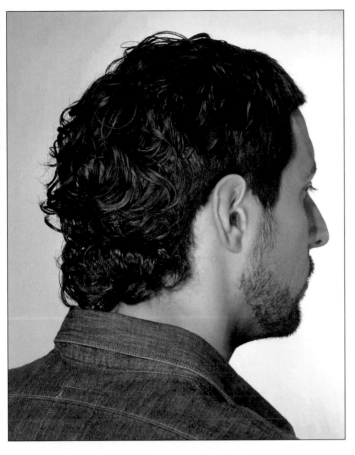

Ladies & Gentlemen Salon & Spa
HAIR: Katie Baxter for Ladies & Gentlemen Salon & Spa, Cleveland, OH
PHOTO: Tom Carson

Ladies & Gentlemen Salon & Spa
HAIR: Jennifer Juratovac for Ladies & Gentlemen Salon & Spa, Cleveland, OH
PHOTO: Tom Carson

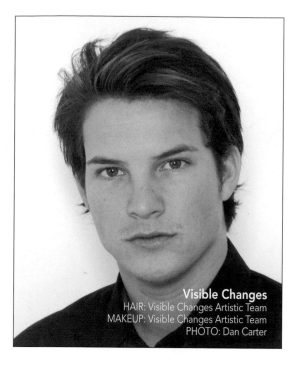

Visible Changes
HAIR: Visible Changes Artistic Team
MAKEUP: Visible Changes Artistic Team
PHOTO: Dan Carter

Rudy and Kelly Battlefield
HAIR: Courtney Gomia
MAKEUP: Courtney Gomia
PHOTO: Davood Salek

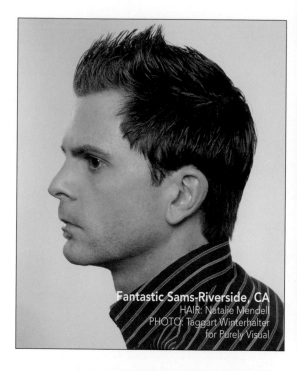

Fantastic Sams-Riverside, CA
HAIR: Natalie Mendell
PHOTO: Taggart Winterhalter
for Purely Visual

HBL Hair Care
HAIR: Patrick Dockry
MAKEUP: Keesh Winkler-Smith
PHOTO: Allen Carrasco

T Hair Design Sarl
HAIR: Artistique Team T. Hair
PHOTO: Yves Kortum

**Von Kekel
Aveda Salon Spa**
HAIR: Krystal Rodriguez
PHOTO: Tom Carson

Pilo Arts Salon & Spa N.Y.C.
HAIR: Mohammad Almaaly
COLOR: Mohammad Almaaly
MAKEUP: Suzanne Alfonso
PHOTO: Photography Elite Inc.

**Cutting Loose
Salon & Spa**
HAIR: Coral Pleas
PHOTO: Tom Carson

**Von Kekel
Aveda Salon Spa**
HAIR: Shawn Von Kekel
PHOTO: Tom Carson

**Expressions
a Salon**
HAIR: Ray Tompkins
PHOTO: Nicole Pena

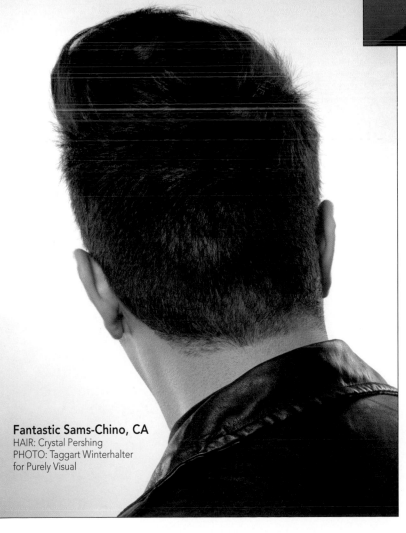

Fantastic Sams-Chino, CA
HAIR: Crystal Pershing
PHOTO: Taggart Winterhalter
for Purely Visual

Anása Hair Studio
HAIR: Helen Botsis
MAKEUP: Jaimie Queenen
PHOTO: Taggart Winterhalter
for Purely Visual

**Ladies & Gentlemen
Salon & Spa**
HAIR: Katie Baxter for
Ladies & Gentlemen Salon
& Spa, Cleveland, OH
PHOTO: Tom Carson

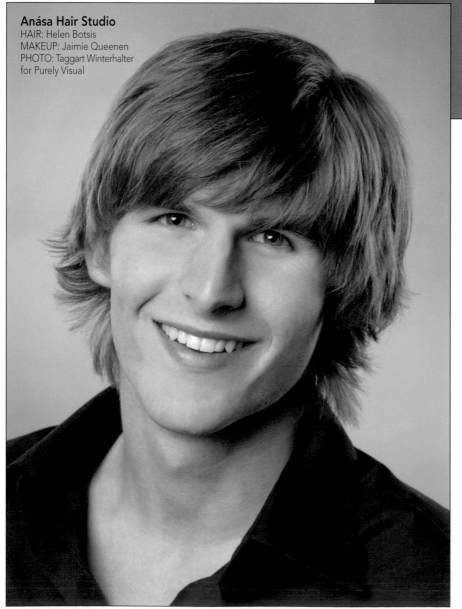

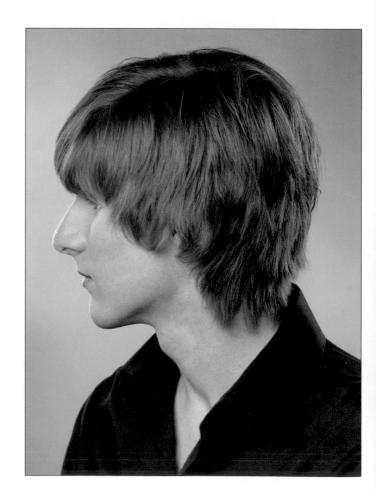

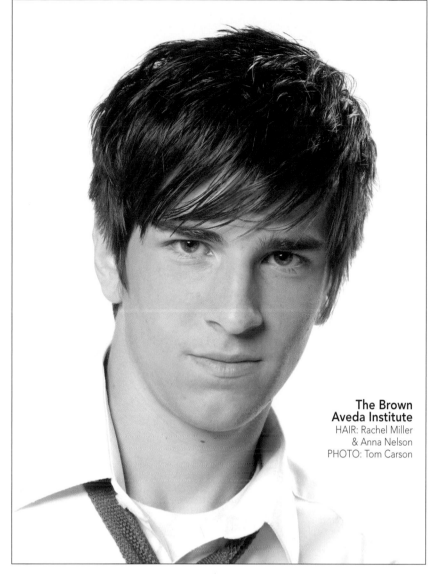

**The Brown
Aveda Institute**
HAIR: Rachel Miller
& Anna Nelson
PHOTO: Tom Carson

ENJOY Hair Care
HAIR: Angel Del Solar & Patrick Dockry
COLOR: Tawny Pierce & Katie Petta
MAKEUP: Keesch Winkler-Smith
PHOTO: Allen Carrasco

**Simply Swank
Salon & Spa**
HAIR: Valerie Hennis
PHOTO: Tom Carson

Visions of Hair Inc.
HAIR: Letisha Harper
MAKEUP: Daylee Clark
PHOTO: Jason Petrillo

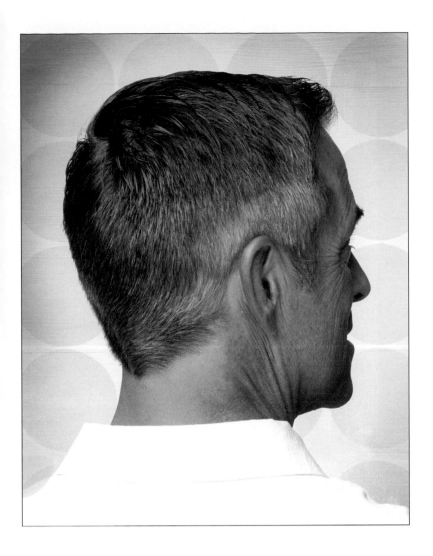

D'Amand Salon & Day Spa
HAIR: Paula Sabins
MAKEUP: Kathleen Clarkson
PHOTO: Tom Carson

Fantastic Sams
Chino, CA
HAIR: Jeanette Contreras
PHOTO: Taggart Winterhalter
for Purely Visual

Fantastic Sams
Norco,CA
HAIR: Linda Morrell
PHOTO: Taggart Winterhalter
for Purely Visual

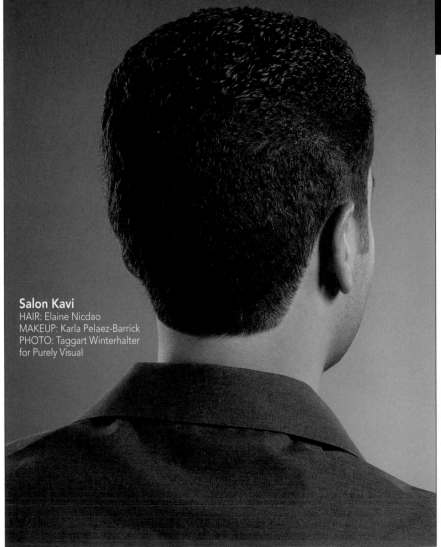

Salon Kavi
HAIR: Elaine Nicdao
MAKEUP: Karla Pelaez-Barrick
PHOTO: Taggart Winterhalter
for Purely Visual

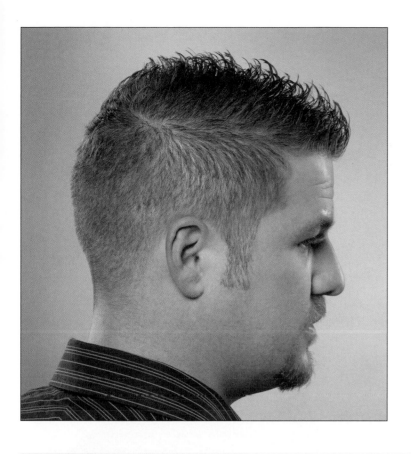

Fantastic Sams
Corona, CA
HAIR: Magda Nieblas
PHOTO: Taggart Winterhalter
for Purely Visual

Art of Hair
HAIR: Jessica Bowen
MAKEUP: Sara Wayne
PHOTO:
Taggart Winterhalter
for Purely Visual

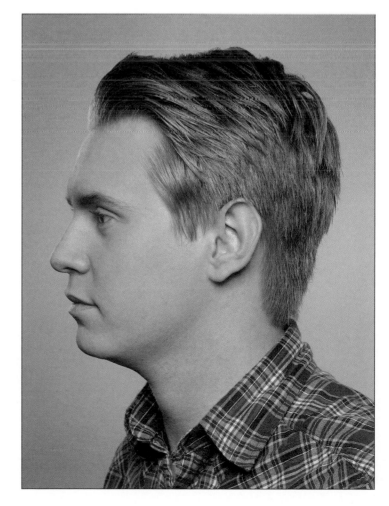

Fantastic Sams
Huntington Beach, CA
HAIR: Elizabeth Strohecker
PHOTO: Taggart Winterhalter
for Purely Visual

Ladies & Gentlemen
Salon & Spa
HAIR: Michael Pavlick for
Ladies & Gentlemen
Salon & Spa, Cleveland, OH
PHOTO: Tom Carson

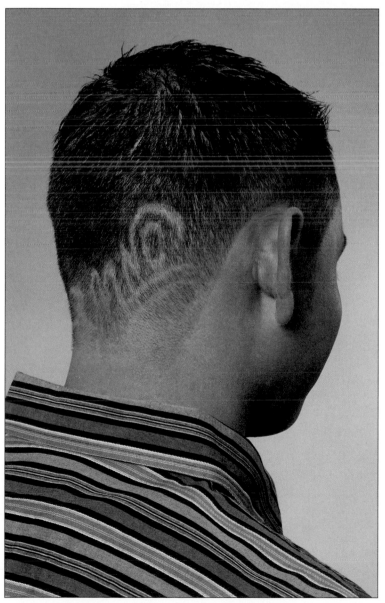

Fantastic Sams
Corona, CA
HAIR: Magda Nieblas
PHOTO: Taggart Winterhalter
for Purely Visual

ENJOY Hair Care
HAIR: Tawny Pierce
MAKEUP: Keesch Winkler-Smith
PHOTO: Allen Carrasco

Ladies & Gentlemen Salon & Spa
HAIR: Stacey Hubrath for Ladies & Gentlemen Salon & Spa, Cleveland, OH
PHOTO: Tom Carson

Visible Changes
HAIR: Visible Changes Artistic Team
MAKEUP: Visible Changes Artistic Team
PHOTO: Dan Carter

Victor Paul Salon
HAIR: Jaymee Poole
MAKEUP: Selina Lopez
PHOTO: Taggart Winterhalter
for Purely Visual

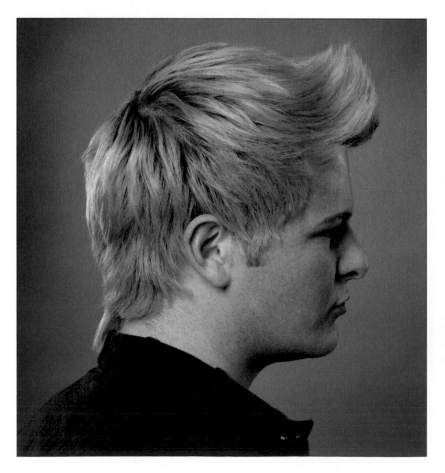

Fantastic Sams
Corona, CA
HAIR: Ashley Johnson
PHOTO: Taggart Winterhalter
for Purely Visual

Diadema Hair Fashion
HAIR: X-men
MAKEUP: Cristina Marzo per Diadema
PHOTO: Stefano Bidini

Fantastic Sams
Lake Elsinore, CA
HAIR: Yazmin Lopez
PHOTO: Taggart
Winterhalter
for Purely Visual

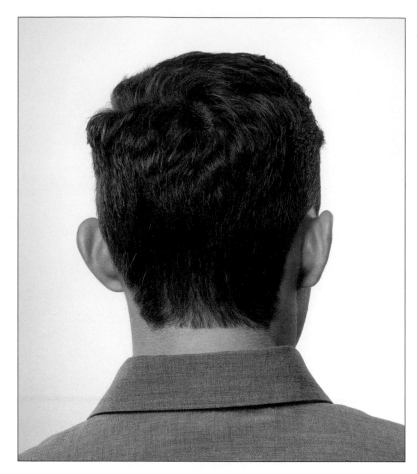

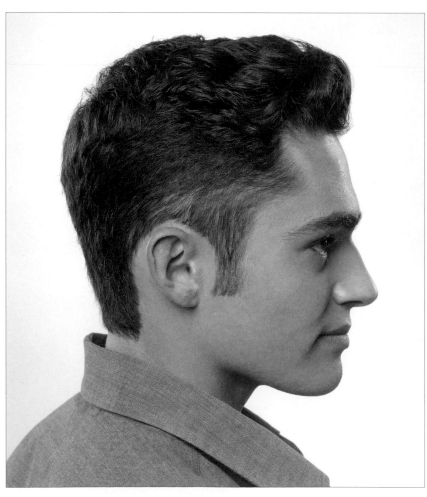

Fantastic Sams
Lake Elsinore, CA
HAIR: Yazmin Lopez
PHOTO: Taggart
Winterhalter
for Purely Visual

Fantastic Sams
Riverside, CA
HAIR: Britain Richards
PHOTO: Taggart Winterhalter
for Purely Visual

Fantastic Sams
Ontario, CA
HAIR: Miriam Palacios
PHOTO: Taggart
Winterhalter
for Purely Visual

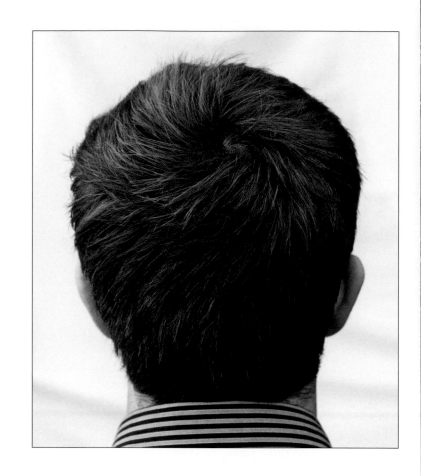

Belleza
HAIR: Regina Zaouk
COLOR: Regina Zaouk
MAKEUP: Chris Smith
PHOTO: Meghan Francis

Art of Hair
HAIR: Summer Vindedahl
MAKEUP: Jaime Queenin
PHOTO: Taggart Winterhalter
for Purely Visual

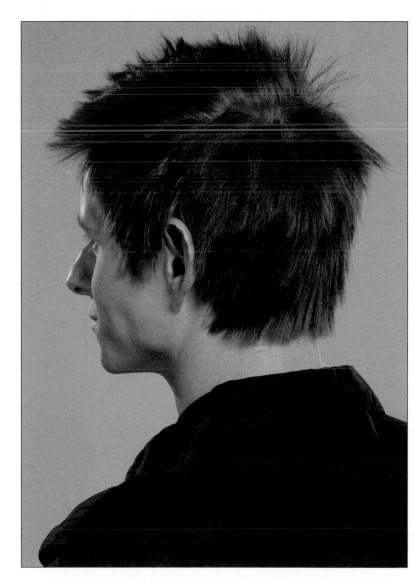

MEN'S STYLES

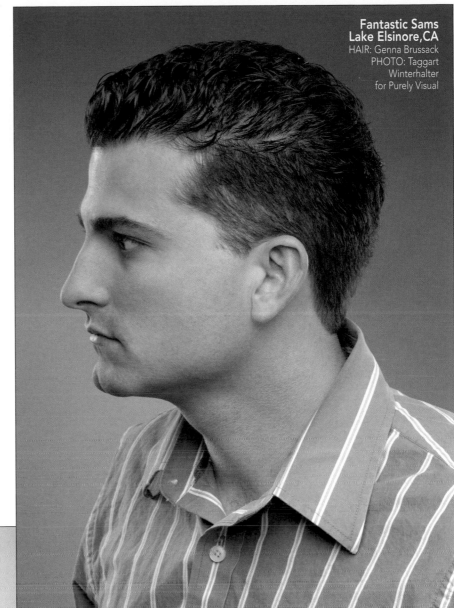

**Fantastic Sams
Lake Elsinore,CA**
HAIR: Genna Brussack
PHOTO: Taggart
Winterhalter
for Purely Visual

Fantastic Sams-Brea, CA
HAIR: Vanessa Valadez
PHOTO: Taggart Winterhalter
for Purely Visual

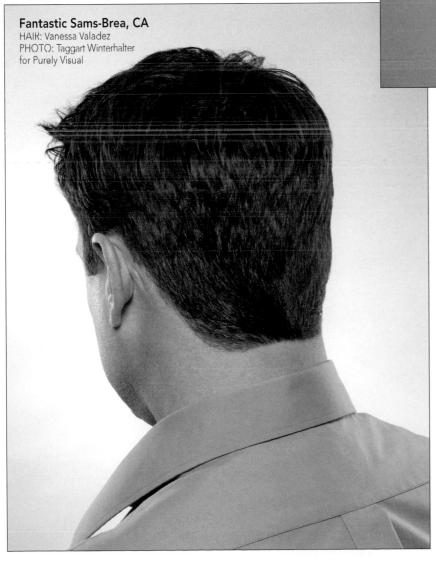

Visible Changes
HAIR: Visible Changes Artistic Team
MAKEUP: Visible Changes Artistic Team
PHOTO: Dan Carter

Belleza
HAIR: Kira Myers
COLOR: Kira Myers
MAKEUP: Andi
Satterfield
PHOTO: Meghan
Francis

Salon Renaissance
HAIR: Debra Barnard
MAKEUP: Debra Barnard
PHOTO: Matt Deverman,
Chris Deverman

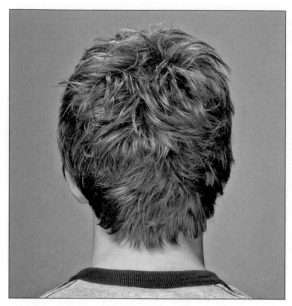

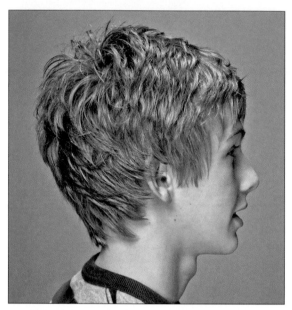

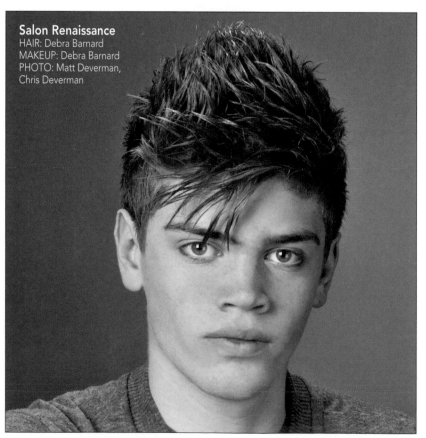

Salon Renaissance
HAIR: Debra Barnard
MAKEUP: Debra Barnard
PHOTO: Matt Deverman,
Chris Deverman

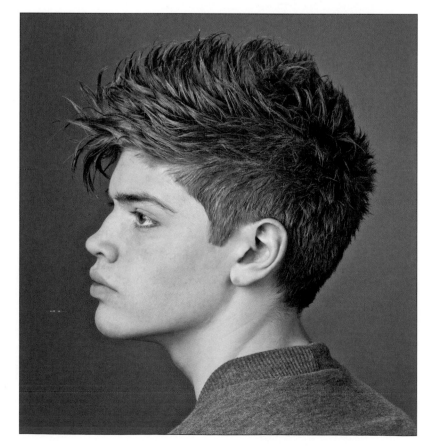

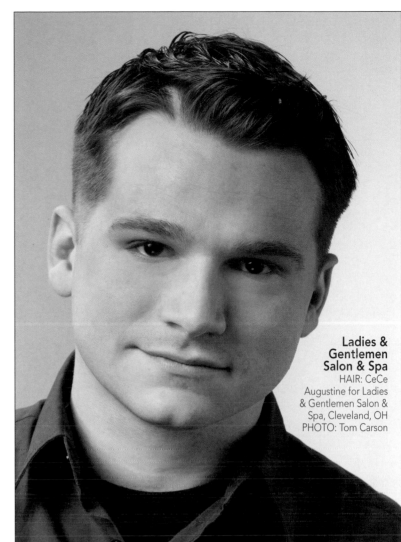

Ladies & Gentlemen Salon & Spa
HAIR: CeCe Augustine for Ladies & Gentlemen Salon & Spa, Cleveland, OH
PHOTO: Tom Carson

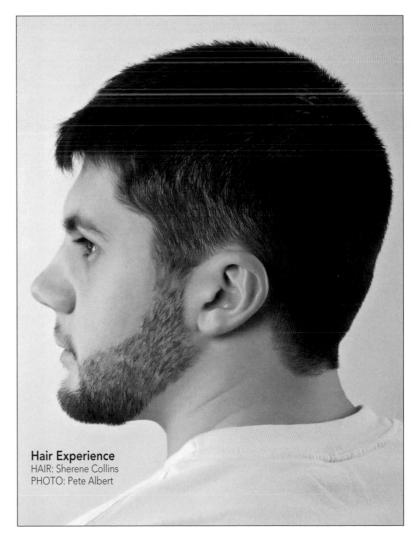

Hair Experience
HAIR: Sherene Collins
PHOTO: Pete Albert

Ladies & Gentlemen
Salon & Spa
HAIR: Katie Baxter for
Ladies & Gentlemen Salon
& Spa, Cleveland, OH
PHOTO: Tom Carson

Ladies & Gentlemen
Salon & Spa
HAIR: Michael Pavlick for
Ladies & Gentlemen Salon
& Spa, Cleveland, OH
PHOTO: Tom Carson

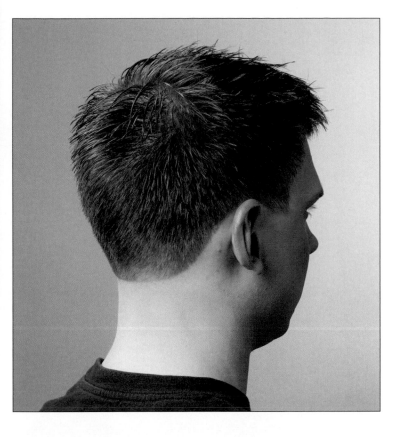

Ladies & Gentlemen Salon & Spa
HAIR: Katie Reis for Ladies & Gentlemen
Salon & Spa, Cleveland, OH
PHOTO: Tom Carson

Fantastic Sams
Riverside, CA
HAIR: Elizabeth Frazier
PHOTO: Taggart
Winterhalter
for Purely Visual

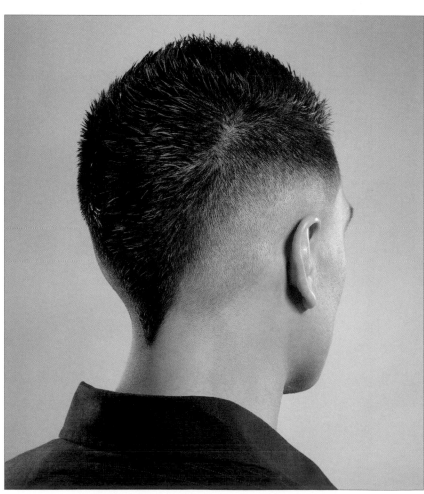

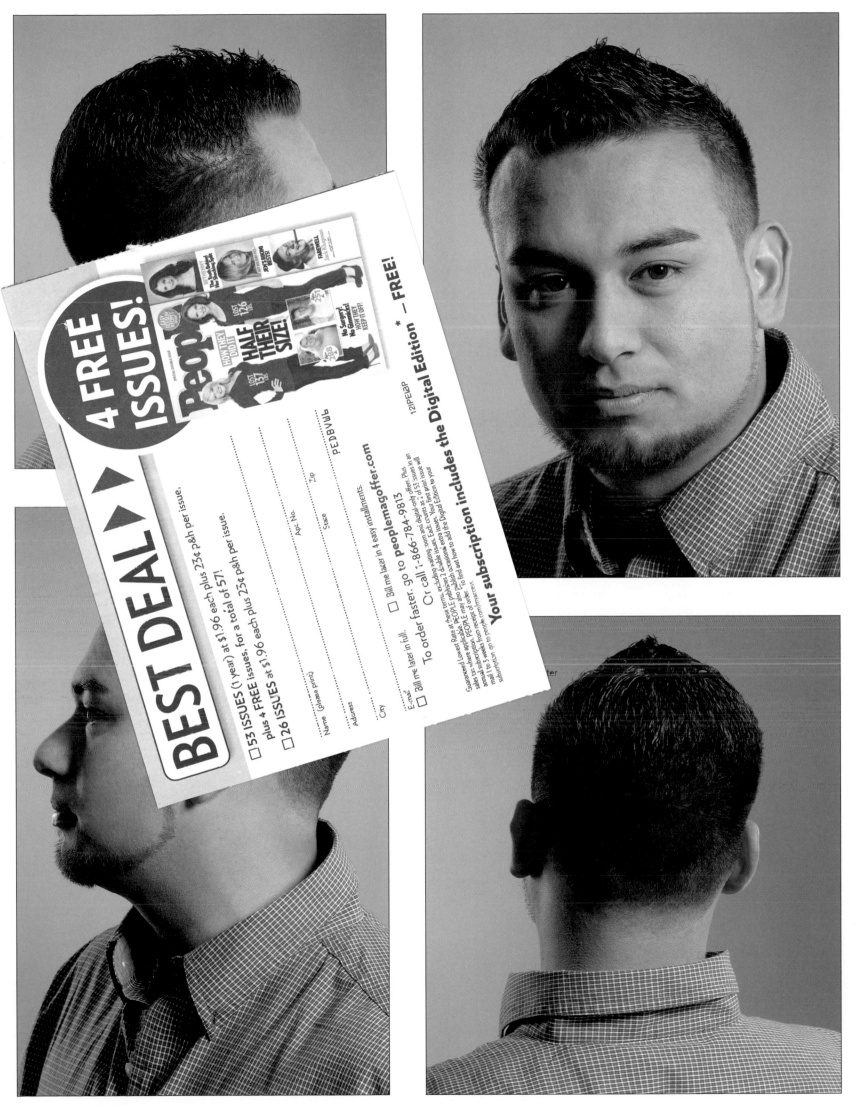

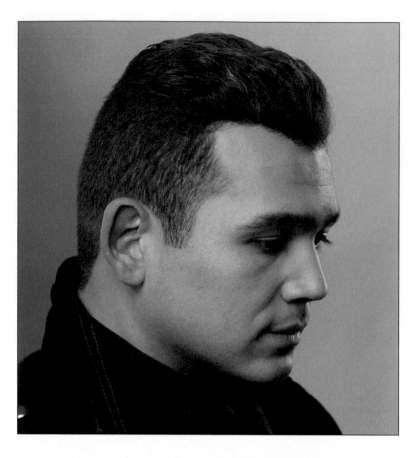

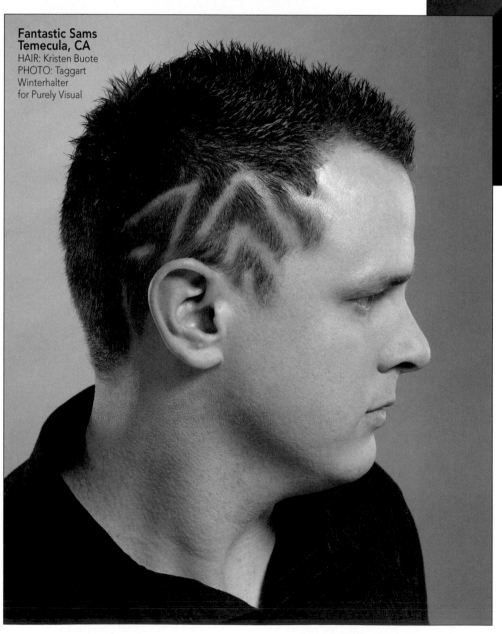

Scruples Professional
Salon Products, Inc.
HAIR: Mia Liguori McHugh
MAKEUP: Ronda Jackson
PHOTO: Jake Armor

Auriginal Designs
HAIR: Aurilla Goldsmith
PHOTO: Fels Andermathes,
Fels Photo & Retouch

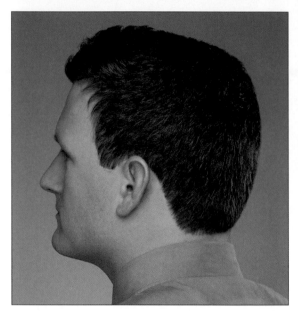

What's New The Salon
HAIR: Karina Kingsnorth
PHOTO: Daphayne Chrisman

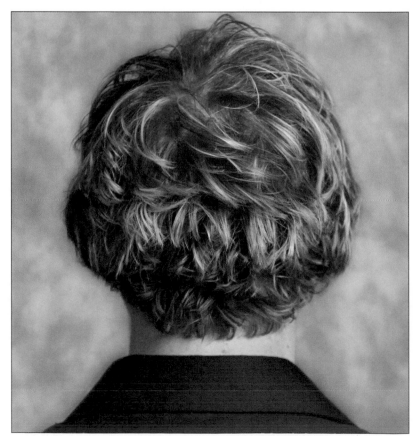

**Strawberry
Fields Spálon**
HAIR: Franco Carolla
MAKEUP: Jeimy Garcia
PHOTO: Noelle
Mitchell Photographix

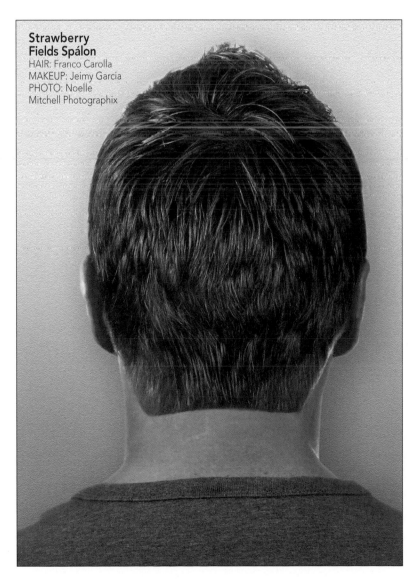

Fantastic Sams
Corona, CA
HAIR: Gregoria Villalobos
PHOTO: Taggart Winterhalter
for Purely Visual

J.Garza Hair Designs
HAIR: Jimmy Garza
MAKEUP: Jimmy Garza
PHOTO: Jay Salazar,
Southwest Photographics

**Ladies & Gentlemen
Salon & Spa**
HAIR: Michael Pavlick for
Ladies & Gentlemen
Salon & Spa, Cleveland, OH
PHOTO: Tom Carson

Visions of Hair Inc.
HAIR: Letisha Harper
MAKEUP: Dayloc Clark
PHOTO: Jason Petrillo

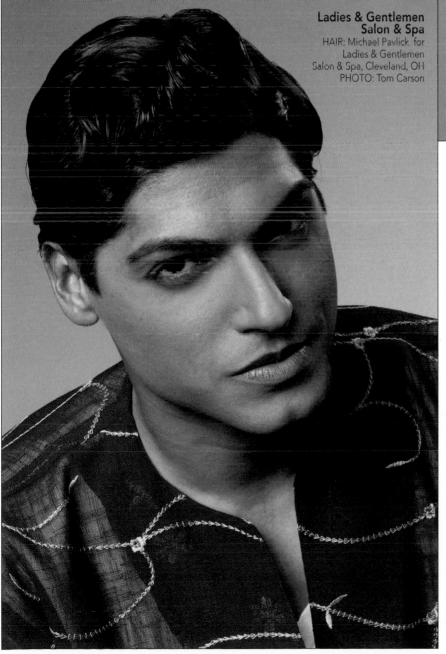

Claiborne's Salon
HAIR: Claiborne's
Design Team
MAKEUP: Claiborne's
Design Team
PHOTO: Oma Cain

Salon Solei
HAIR: Tina Reinders
COLOR: Jasmine Koch
MAKEUP: Ashlee Gassert
PHOTO: Rita Backus

New York
New York Salon
HAIR: Sheri Ritchey
COLOR: Sheri Ritchey
MAKEUP: Lacey Powell
PHOTO: Henry Duncan

New York
New York Salon
HAIR: Kimberly Nigh
COLOR: Kimberly Nigh
MAKEUP: Lacey Powell
PHOTO: Henry Duncan

Visible Changes
HAIR: Visible Changes Artistic Team
MAKEUP: Visible Changes Artistic Team
PHOTO: Teddy Tran

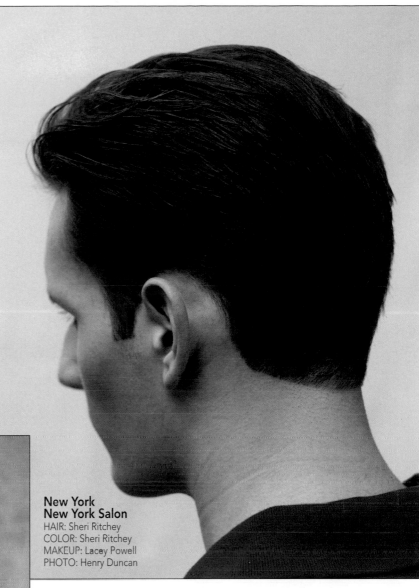

**New York
New York Salon**
HAIR: Sheri Ritchey
COLOR: Sheri Ritchey
MAKEUP: Lacey Powell
PHOTO: Henry Duncan

**Fantastic Sams
Corona, CA**
HAIR: Rosalind Pacleb
PHOTO: Taggart Winterhalter
for Purely Visual

Channing Tatum
PHOTO: Lester Cohen/
WireImage

Channing Tatum
PHOTO: Jon Kopaloff/
FilmMagic

Paul Rudd
PHOTO: Frazer Harrison/
Getty Images Entertainment

Paul Rudd
PHOTO: Steve Granitz/
WireImage

John Hamm
PHOTO: Dave J Hogan/
Getty Images Entertainment

John Hamm
PHOTO: Jeffrey Mayer/
WireImage

Michael C. Hall
PHOTO: Frazer Harrison/
Getty Images Entertainment

Bradley Cooper
PHOTO: Kevin Winter /
Getty Images Entertainment

Bradley Cooper
PHOTO: Steve Granitz/
WireImage

Bradley Cooper
PHOTO: George Pimentel/
Getty Images Entertainment

Eric Bana
PHOTO: Vera Anderson/
WireImage

James Franco
PHOTO: Jon Kopaloff/FilmMagic

James Franco
PHOTO: Steve Granitz/WireImage

Hugh Jackman
PHOTO: Jeffrey Mayer/
WireImage

Hugh Jackman
PHOTO: Jason Merritt /
Getty Images
Entertainment

Hugh Jackman
PHOTO: Jon Kopaloff/
FilmMagic

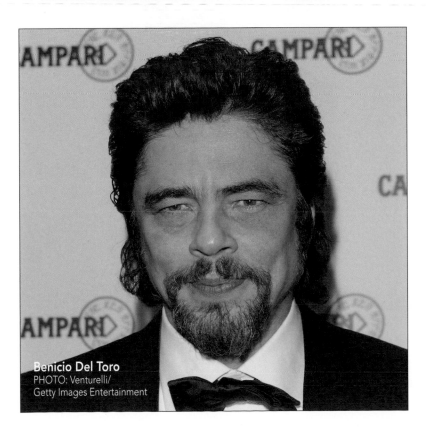

Benicio Del Toro
PHOTO: Venturelli/
Getty Images Entertainment

Benicio Del Toro
PHOTO: Martin Bureau/AFP

Ben Affleck
PHOTO: Stephen Lovekin/
Getty Images
Entertainment

Ben Affleck
PHOTO: Todd Williamson/ WireImage

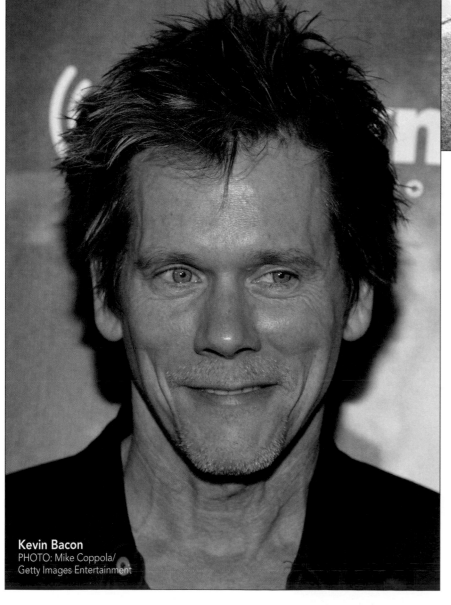

Kevin Bacon
PHOTO: Mike Coppola/
Getty Images Entertainment

Kevin Bacon
PHOTO: Jason LaVeris/
FilmMagic

Bruno Mars
PHOTO: Jason Merritt/Getty Images Entertainment

Matthew Morrison
PHOTO: Jeff Kravitz/FilmMagic, Inc

Matthew Morrison
PHOTO: Frazer Harrison/
Getty Images Entertainment

Matthew Morrison
PHOTO: Jamie McCarthy/
WireImage

Leonardo DiCaprio
PHOTO: Frazer Harrison/Getty Images Entertainment

Leonardo DiCaprio
PHOTO: Steve Granitz / WireImage

Leonardo DiCaprio
PHOTO: Jon Kopaloff/ FilmMagic

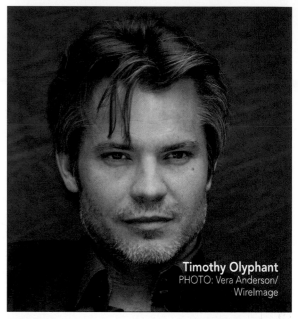

Timothy Olyphant
PHOTO: David Livingston/
Getty Images Entertainment

Timothy Olyphant
PHOTO: Vera Anderson/
WireImage

Geoff Stults
PHOTO: David Livingston/
Getty Images
Entertainment

Johnny Depp
PHOTO: Pascal Le Segretain/
Getty Images Entertainment

Jake Gyllenhaal
PHOTO: Carlos Alvarez/
Getty Images Entertainment

Jake Gyllenhaal
PHOTO: Elisabetta Villa/
Getty Images Entertainment

Publisher/CEO: Deborah Carver • Managing Director: Sheryl Lenzkes • Art Director: Michael Block
To Contact Us: Creative Age Communications • 7628 Densmore Avenue, Van Nuys, California 91406-2042 • PH 800.634.8500 • FAX 818.782.7450
Interested in getting published . . . go to inspirebooks.com to download submission forms and information